ATMOSPHERIC CHAMBERS

+

COLOURWORLD

Recent art by Geoffrey Mark Matthews and Colin Davis

Introduction by Michael Blackburn
Essays by Graham Freestone and Geoffrey Mark Matthews

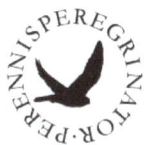

2018

Published by
PERENNISPEREGRINATOR
27 Roman Wharf, Lincoln, LN1 1SN, UK
Atmospheric Chambers and Colourworld Copyright © 2018
Images used with permission.

Design by Geoffrey Mark Matthews
The cover image is used under licence Creative Commons 2.0
adapted from Foam Bubbles. 2. by Adaptalux
<https://www.flickr.com/photos/125216703@N02/16439091900>

ISBN 978-0-9932054-6-0

perennisperegrinator@gmail.com

INTRODUCTION

by Michael Blackburn

One of the great pleasures of encountering Davis and Matthews is that of seeing thoroughly contemporary artists who have absorbed and developed the techniques and approaches of both classical and modern art to produce attractive work that is without the slightest pretentiousness or

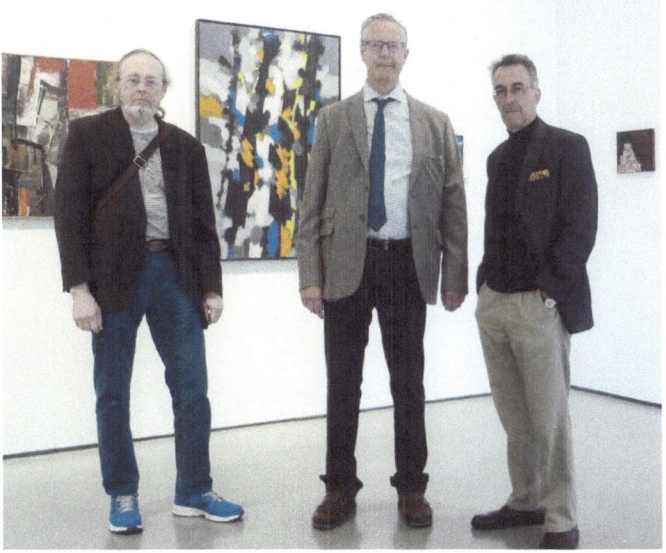

Geoffrey Mark Matthews, Colin Davis and Michael Blackburn on a visit to the Hepworth Gallery, Wakefield, 16 August 2017.

precocity. The images of both artists are striking, thoughtful and provocative. They give you an initial visual hit which then draws you in to consider and reconsider what is going on within the four sides of the image. Davis and Matthews also explore the possibilities of a range of tools and materials:

traditional stick-on collage, acrylic, watercolour, inkjet, hand-made paper, software, and so on.

As the title of Colin Davis's contribution clearly indicates, he is preoccupied with the idea of place (a common obsession with British artists), and where that place is not a real, identifiable one, then one he has imagined—*Cleartown*, obviously, and *Colourworld* itself. It is a very outward-looking, sociable art. Even when the people appear, all wobbly outlines and economically drawn, you get the feeling they are real people metamorphosed into their new environments.

Davis has a firm control of line, which he exploits to full use in these images, and an equally strong appreciation of laying down blocks of colour within those lines. The colours themselves are usually of a rather pastel nature. The effect is striking but not overpowering—in the same way that the lines, always confident, are not necessarily aggressive, but often permit themselves to waver. As a result each image feels as if it were on the verge of starting to move and change in front of your eyes.

What is fascinating is how much of this is achieved using computerised tools. And the feeling that there is a certain comic-book style that transcends the form so that those real people mentioned above, now semi-abstracted, nevertheless retain their human vitality. Even where the images are devoid of human figures you can sense their presence. Above all, there is a freshness to these images, an emotional resonance and a sense of delight in the world around us.

Matthews has really pushed the concept of collage here, melding a variety of techniques to produce works that, on first sight, often appear to be paintings (like those of Davis).

Unlike Davis, though, there's a different vision at work, one that tends to look at the world from the inside out, as it were (it's no surprise that so many include figures of the artist himself) and from a mythological or semi-religious/psychological perspective. The cleverness resides in the fact that most of the images embedded into the collages are drawn from magazines, journals and newspapers—the quotidian is part of the mythological.

This quasi-religious or psychological matter is sometimes seen in the way the collages are subtly divided into upper and lower sections. The upper represents a kind of higher reality, the lower something more decayed and hellish. However, even when you realise this, you are still left with trying to work out what is happening. This is not an art of easy conclusions. It is work that engages with society but on its own terms.

Matthews employs occasionally what I would describe as a comic-book style (like Davis), but transmutes it completely. Many of the images look like they could be posters for bizarre films. There is a brooding, obsessive and dark quality to them; something akin to science fiction. You get the sense that there is some complex narrative underlying them and you are trying to piece the clues together. However much you have worked out, there is still something just out of reach.

Add to this mix the use of text, both as a stand-alone and as something integral visually. The words are gnomic, mysterious, suggestive, generating their own meanings from their juxtapositions, always self-contained in terms of their separate words.

Two very different artists, with very different preoccupations; both using similar techniques, and both producing arresting images. There is enough here to delight the eye and provoke the mind indefinitely

Note.

In the following essays Graham Freestone offers an approach to interpreting Geoffrey Mark Matthews's *Atmospheric Chambers* paintings, and Matthews writes an appreciation of Colin Davis's *Colourworld* project. Illustrations are of work included in the exhibition

TETRA-ANAGRAMMATION

by Graham Freestone

1) This text is a programming of anyone who would read it. It inserts interpretive devices that may or may not improve your experience of the work. It is an exercise in creative interpretation, or textual alchemy (plugging the work into a method to derive further products).

2) The title is derived from the notion of the anagrammatic combined with the 4-letter name of God.

3) 16, as the number of works and the square of 4, hints at the correctness of the God attribution (as a lurking psychic regulator).

4) With any art work the question is the same: How do we find a way in? This of course presupposes there is an in. Surely art is exteriority by definition. But if we do not want to get further *in* why do we grant it our prolonged attention?

5) Some method must be chosen to gain *an* [not *the*] interiority. In this case the 16 images (of the display) were allocated numbers. 4 were selected by divine/arbitrary means.

6) These are the Gates. Their validity as adequate commentary on the whole is guaranteed by the logic of the hologram (any part of it we focus on can reveal something of the totality).

7) The 4 Gates and their numerical attributions are:
   (i) 2: Endgames: ENEMIES OF BLISS.

(ii) 6:: Chrysalis: BUILT AS PROUD LIE—SPIRITUAL DOUBLE—IS TROUBLE LAID UP.

(iii) 12::: Grasping: DESERTED ARCADES—READ DEAD SECRETS.

(iv) 14:::: Resonance: TURBULENT SPHERES—[…].[1]

8) The logic of these 'arbitrary' numbers is not hard to derive. (2) Endgames, the ironic beginning leads in strange circuit to (6) Chrysalis and (12) Grasping. 2*6 gives us the 12 but to have reached the 12 the 6 must have been derived. This is achieved by (12)+=3. This 3 is then multiplied by the 2 to gain the 6. (14) Resonance is achieved by the addition of Endgames (2) to Grasping (12).

9) We note that the work plays with the notion of a 'title' by including textual anagrammation within the images. This subversion of the title enables further decoding in the tension between the two (title and anagrammation).

10) The work is concerned with transformation and translation.

11) Anagrammation is a transformation that alters communication. A medium designed for communicative purpose has its atomic units rearranged.

12) …

---

[1] The anagram Graham failed to perceive is: SUBTLE SPURN THERE. (GMM)

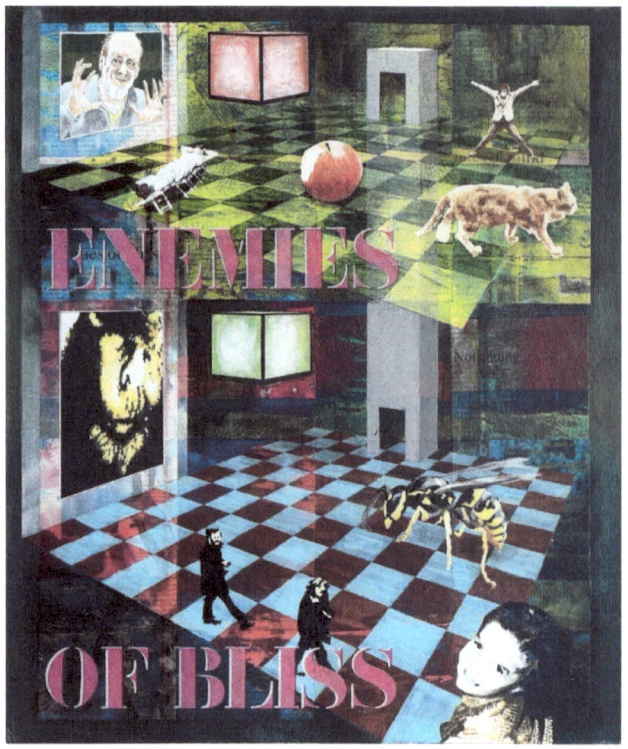

Endgames (2017)
Collage and acrylic on canvas board 608 x 508.

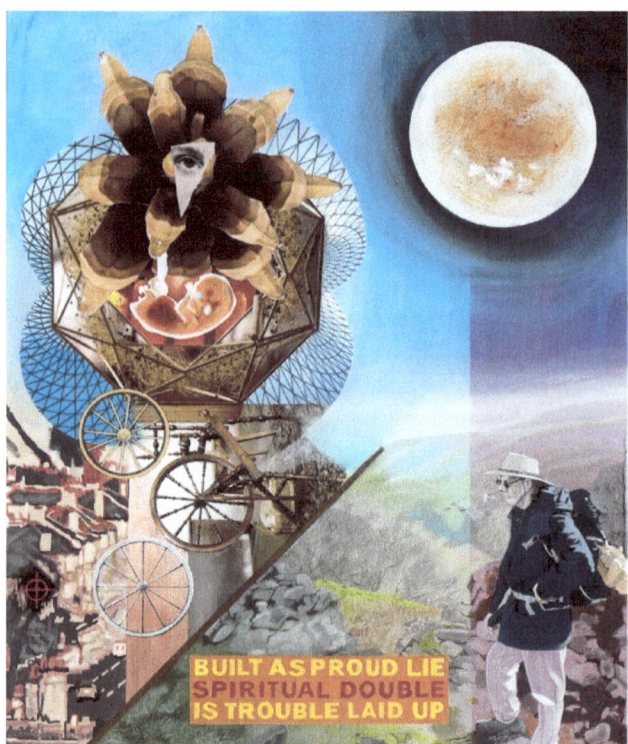

Chrysalis (2018)
Acrylic, collage and ink on canvas board 608 x 508.

Gate 1: Endgames

The double is a feature of the series. The series is embedded in the primal double 1*2. Like Sloterdijk's *Spheres* it starts with 2. This image screams the double at us. The double floor, the double cube, the double grey fireplace-like structure, the cat-wasp. The double window—which displays below something I intuited at first as a mandrill and above the demonic artist at the window, emblematic of another double, the doppelgänger (where is the real artist?) Only the Erisian apple, St. Andrew, the

girl (is there a shade of the demonic there too?) and the sleeping one escape this logic.

Gate 2: Chrysalis.

The words of Gate 2 tell us the double is still manifest. The spiritual double is shown in the emblematic God eye entity in its relation to the Christ foetus. Yet this double intimates its existence predicated on a geometric order behind it or encapsulating it: The Chris[t]alis: the perfect medium of transformation and concealment: the wholly pneuma. God is after the fact not before it, intimating a dialectic resolution. This making three is shown too by the triple anagram. The hiker-artist displays a Zen like quality, unmoved by the transcendent reality just beyond the twilight. The twilight is outside of this realm—it occupies approximately a fifth of the canvas, leaving a totality of *four* equal parts. The hiker-twilight is in a sense

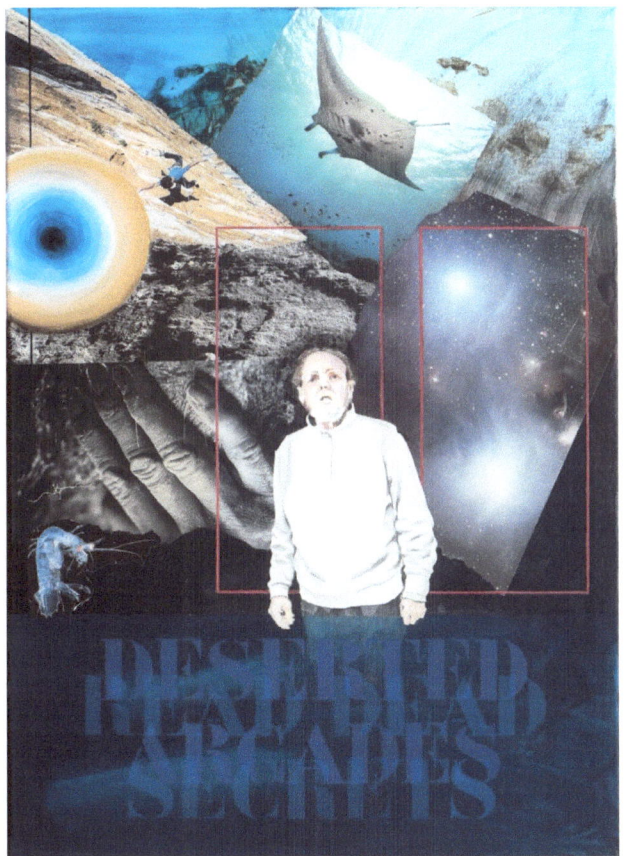

Grasping (2017)
Acrylic, collage and ink on canvas 700 x 500.

not part of the same order. Moon—a well-known duality symbol connects the *two* [worlds]. Is the doppelgänger the true self or is not the Zen-self the true self? The doppelgänger that appears as demonic is the everyday *enemy of bliss*. The Zen character is empty and outside the doubling series but connected to it (twilight—he is between).

Gate 3: Grasping

Reconciliation of the doppelgänger and the Zen-self leave the angst-riddled protagonist emerging from an abyss (the empty double window reinforces this interpretation). The peaceful Zen hiker is replaced with the struggle of the climb. The climbing hand displays four digits (the hand of God). The sphere has become a collapsing in on its own emptiness. The self is perceived, from the failed grasp, to fulfil its emptiness (this is the essential *grasping*). The anagrammatic formula says it all: DESERTED ARCADES—READ DEAD SECRETS. The emptiness of the arcade—itself a series of arched ways, of emptinesses. Read secrets that themselves have died—a dead secret is in the open; it is no longer secret. The secret of the self is no longer secret. The structure that specialises in emptiness is deserted. Has the Man-drill become a Man-ta ray?

Gate 4: Resonance

There is a desire to know the key to TURBULENT SPHERES but it will not come. [This in itself is a clue—concealment]. The work has been

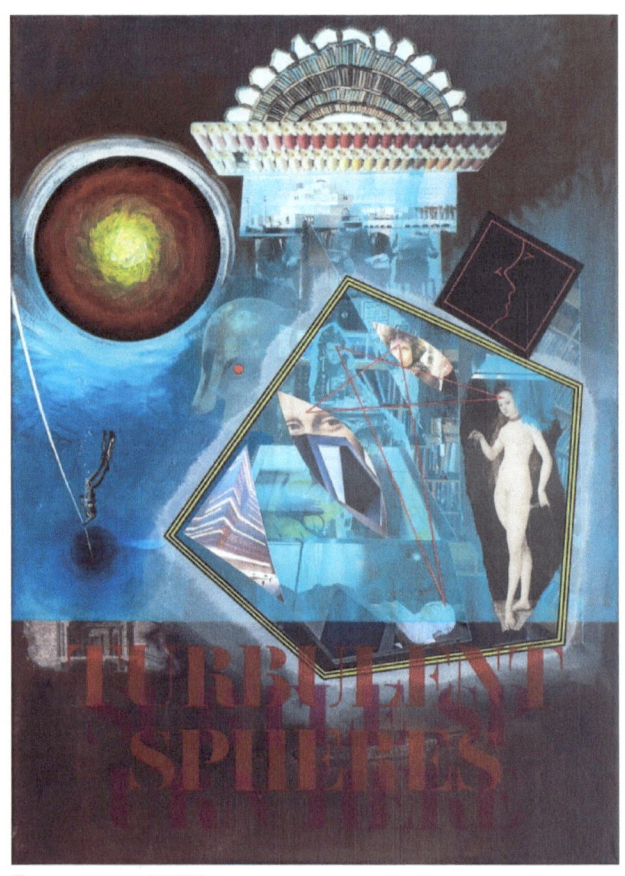

Resonance (2017)
Acrylic, collage and ink on canvas 700 x 500.

transformed (translated) from plane to plane. The climb leads down but the diver descends up. The sphere above shows from whence he came (the dark point of the last sphere). Now in the realm of the temple or the *reel* (remember St Andrew—he rules over rope makers) the double has lost its power. The upright irregular pentagon containing the inverted irregular pentagram (suggestive of the law of fives and esotericism): the triumph of pneuma over matter followed by its opposite. The sequence of eyes within indicates how doubling takes place within as part of a *process*. Tetra-anagrammation occurs exactly here: Two Venuses [?] (Queen and Princess), two Dylans [?] (King and Prince) and *something* that might be the swaddling of the Christ-foetus. Most key (the key?) to it all is that the protagonist-artist has vanished. The interiority is *not* silent, it is just reality deified.

Exits Exist

Each image is filled with other exit points that lead to new Gates. *Enumeration is meaningless.*

ATMOSPHERIC CHAMBERS

Geoffrey Mark Matthews

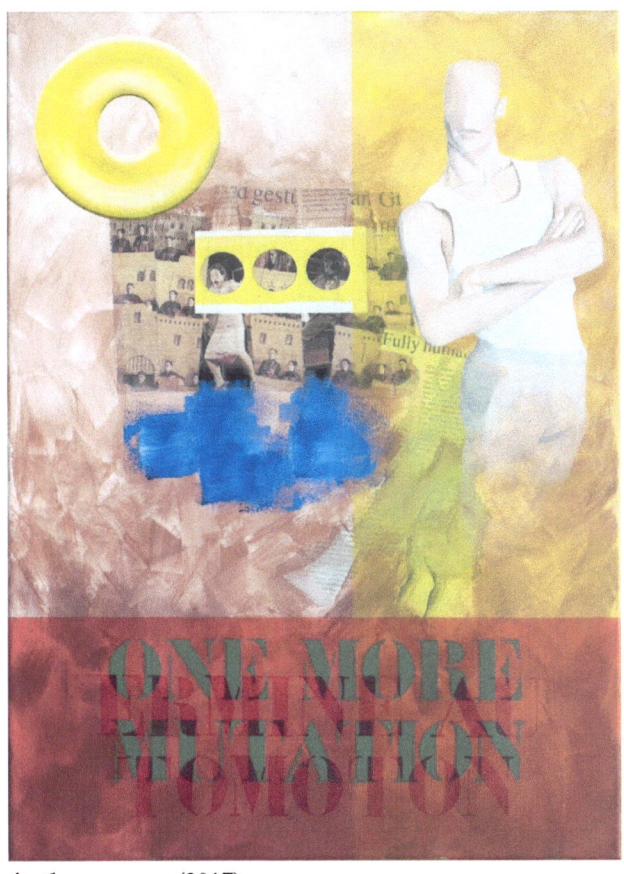

Anthropocene (2017)
Acrylic and collage on canvas 700 x 500.

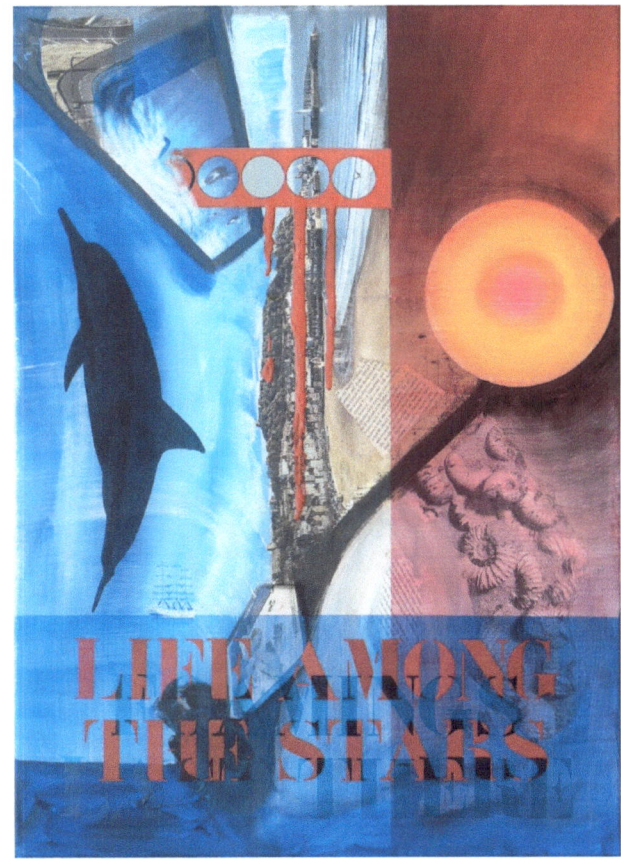

Ammonite Dreams (2017)
Acrylic and collage on canvas 700 x 500.

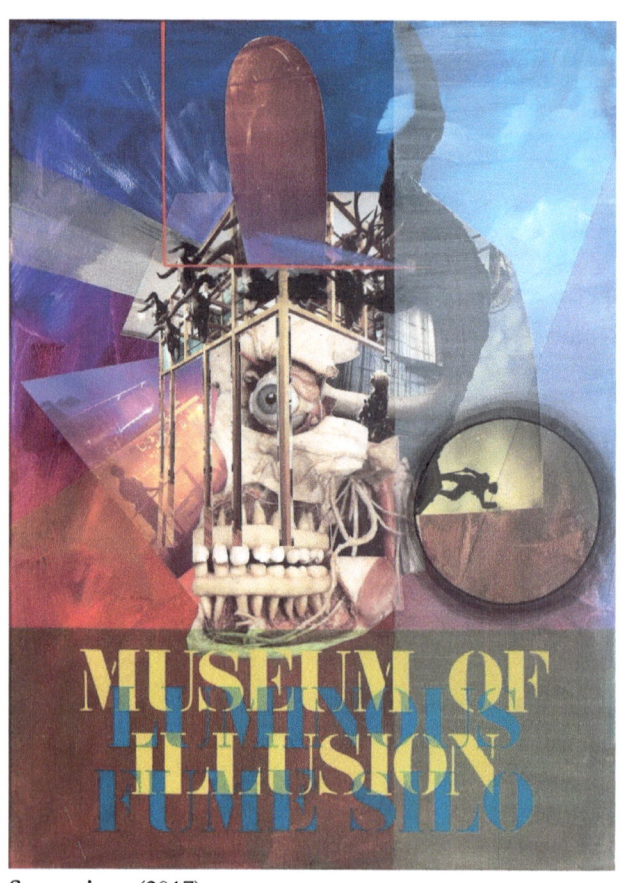

Sensorium (2017)
Acrylic and collage on canvas 700 x 500.

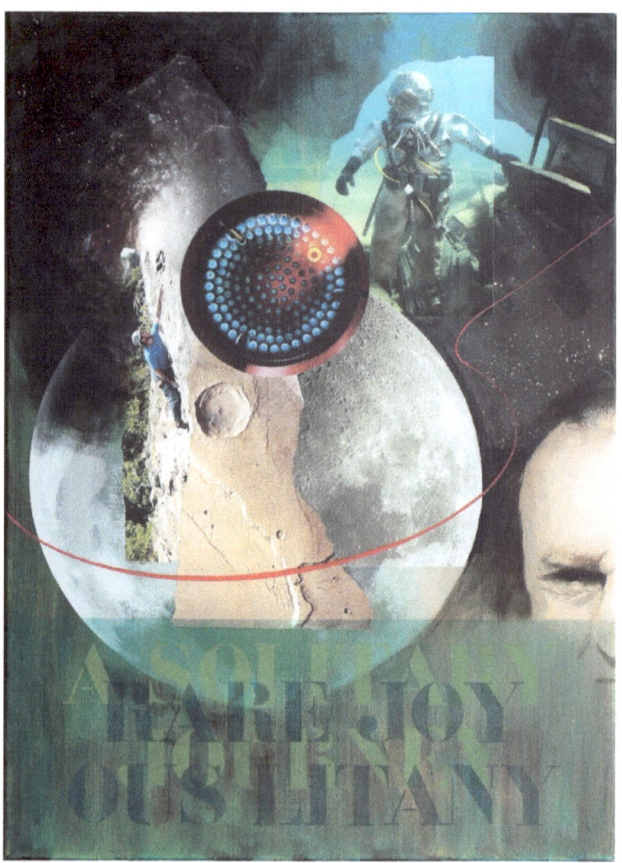

Roundabout (2017)
Acrylic and collage on canvas 700 x 500.

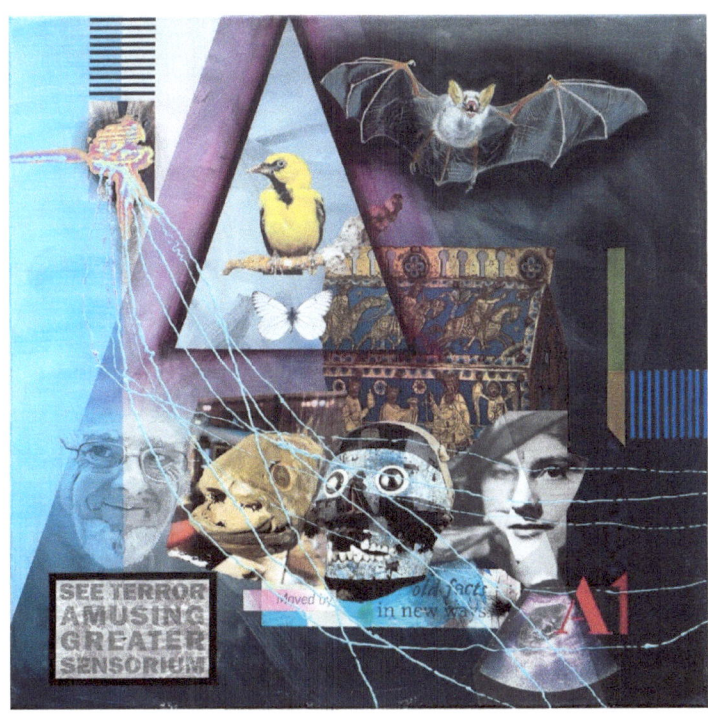

Invasion of Novelty (2018)
Acrylic, collage, aluminium foil and ink on canvas 600 x 600.

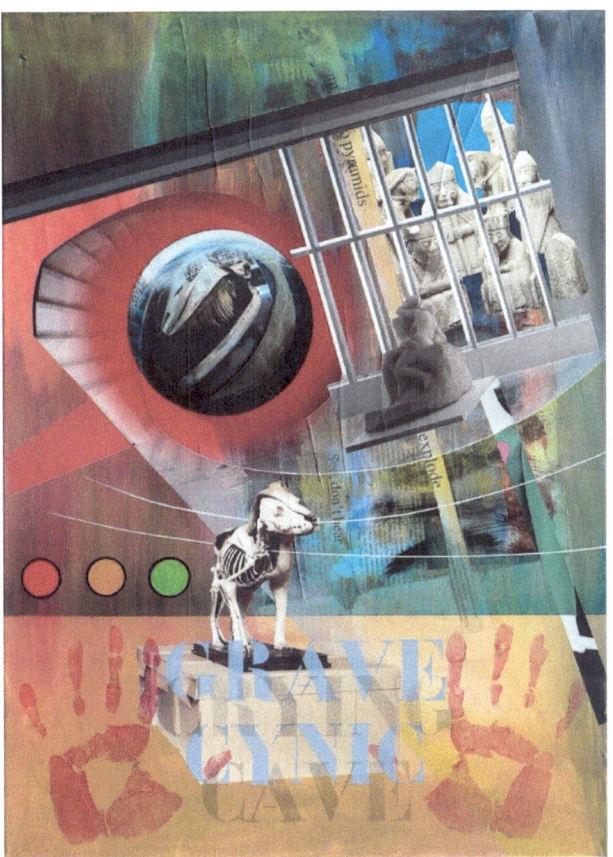

Insula (2017)
Acrylic and collage on canvas 700 x 500.

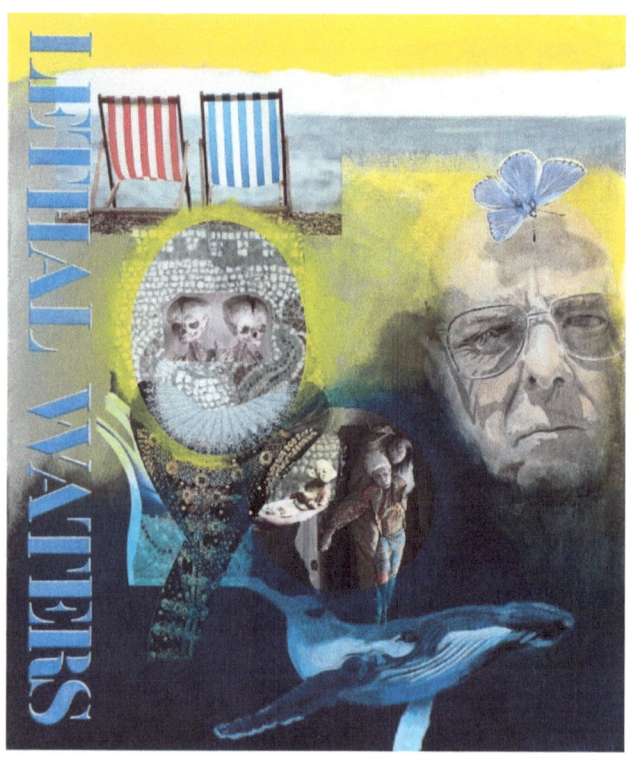

Hypnos and Thanatos (2017)
Acrylic and collage on canvas board 608 x 508.

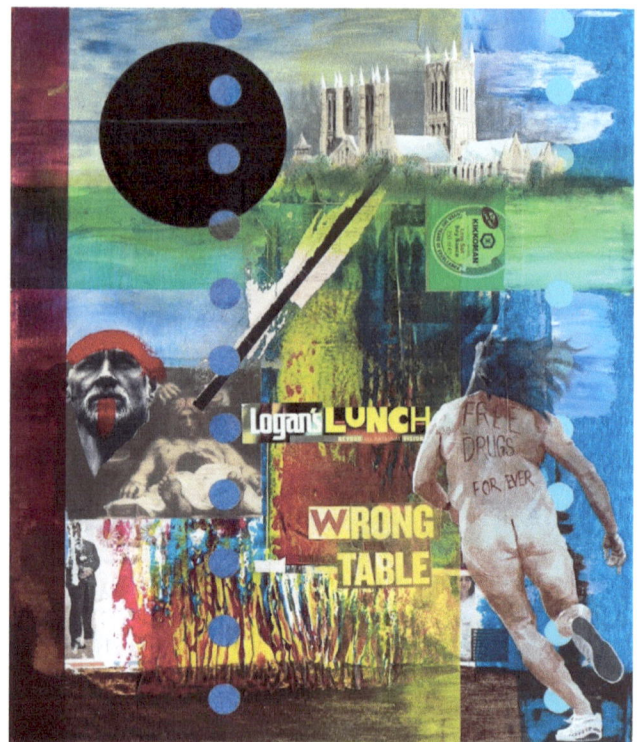

Sojourn (2017)
Acrylic and collage on canvas board 610 x 508.

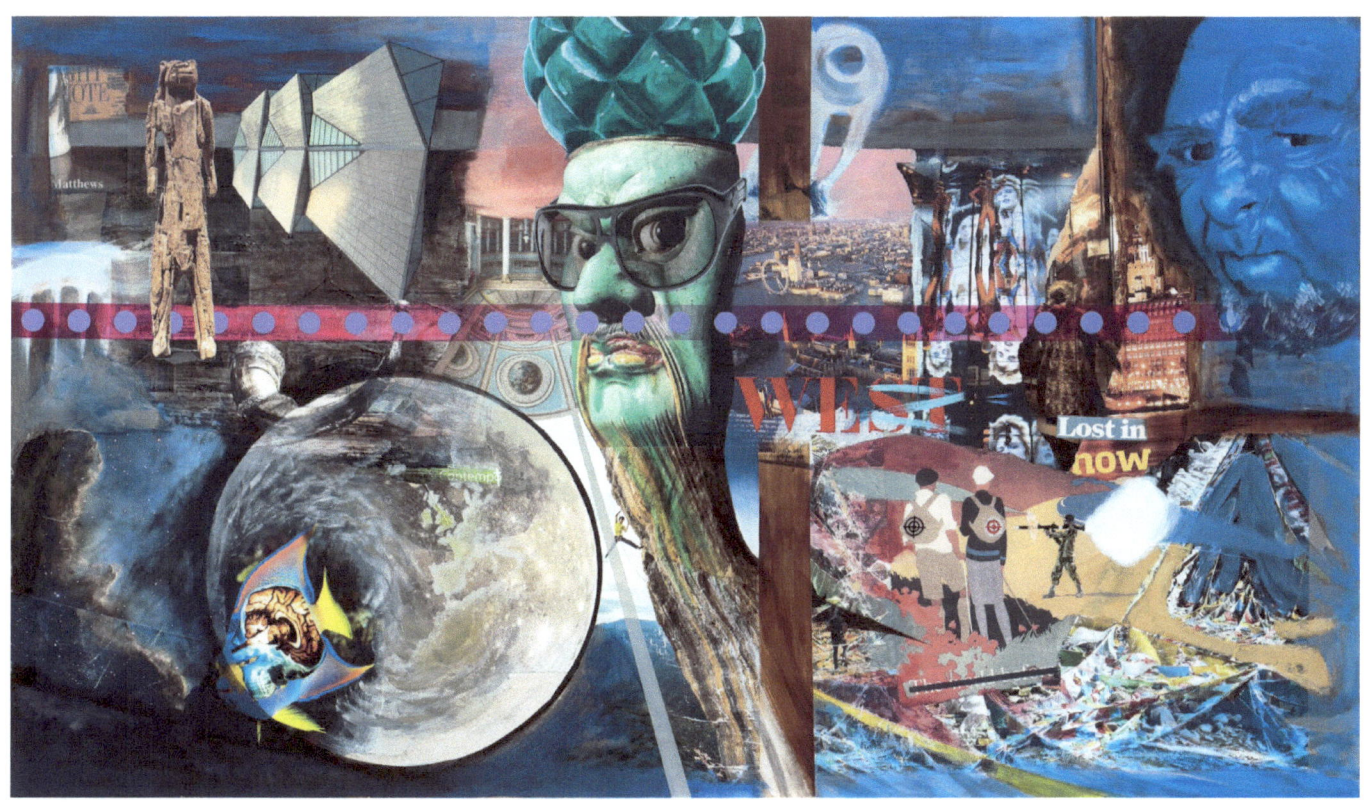

Lost in Now (2017)
Acrylic, collage, ink and graphite on hardboard 710 x 1220.

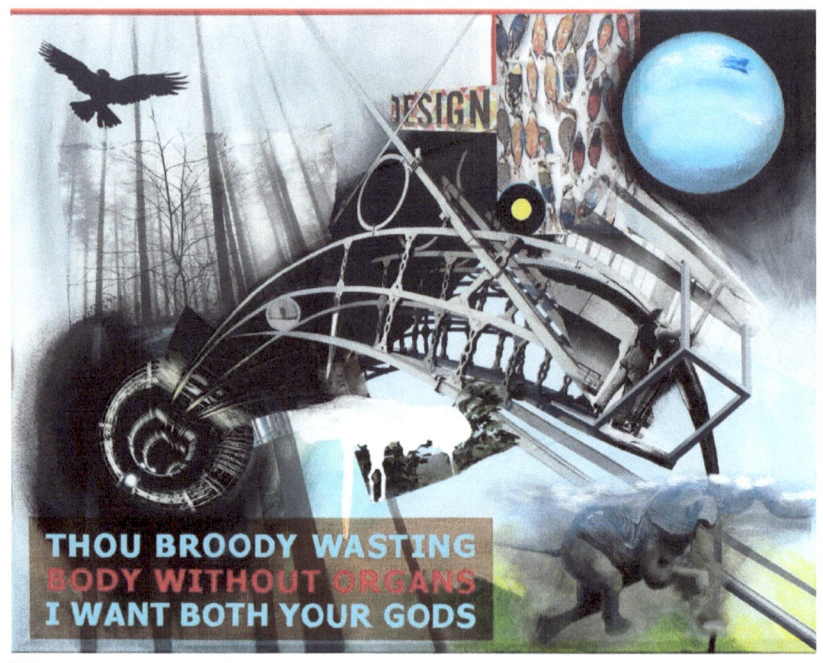

Therapeutics (2018)
Acrylic, collage and graphite on canvas 610 x 762.

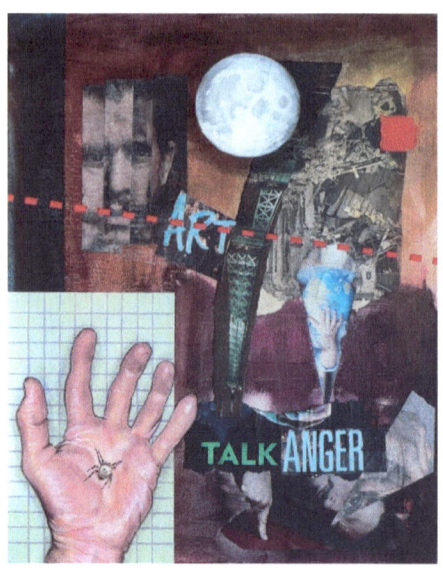

Negre Cave (2017)
Acrylic and collage on hardboard 633 x 406.

Resurgence (2018)
Acrylic and collage on canvas board 455 x 355.

COLOURWORLD ADVENTURE

by Geoffrey Mark Matthews

If one is to approach Colin Davis's recent work fairly I believe that the core consideration should be not so much 'the way of seeing the world' as 'the world that is seen.' Although he professes and demonstrates a painterly concern for material and its

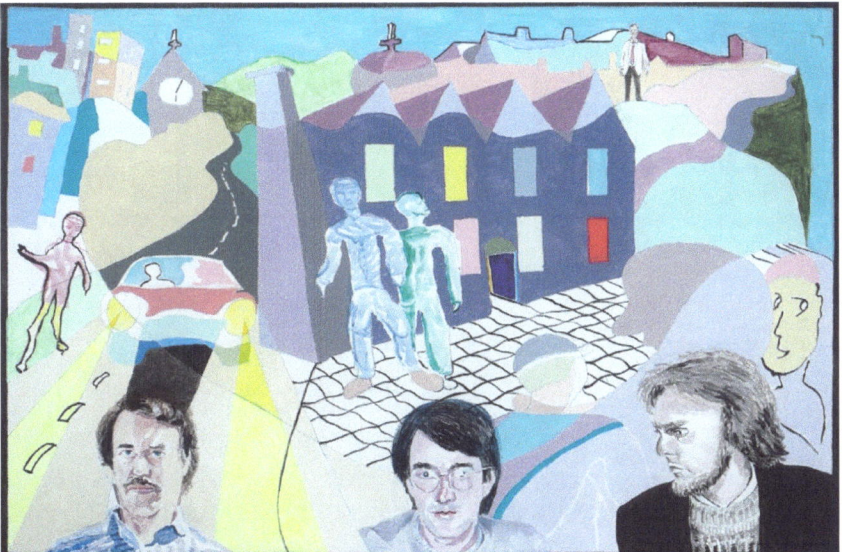

Three Lads from the North (2017)
Acrylic on canvas 510 x 760.

use in translating a vision, the more important dimension for Davis is the vision itself which is an adventure into a personal mythology of origins. Origins of place, of culture, of relationship, and of meaning, emerge in the gloriously colour-filled world of his invention. He calls it *Colourworld* and in

it, scene by scene, his vision opens up through the engagement of memory and imagination in a dance with reality.

The people in Davis's paintings are his friends and family, real individuals whose representation reimagines them as characters animating a setting. They are like players who strut their stuff. But they do so not to tell stories. Any past events depicted in these scenes are biographically incidental and historically trivial such that no message is intended from either of those points of view. Rather, the characters act as markers in the territory, as signs of life, and as devices in a world machine. As such I interpret them as the generators of energy peculiar to each moment. The nature of the 'peculiar' in the moment is what is important because it is something that the artist invents.

When an artist says, 'this is how I see things,' it is a statement about fact and about process. It is almost always a mistake to assume that it concerns the success of a particular work, even if, as sometimes happens, the artist makes such a claim. The reason why the phrase is important then is

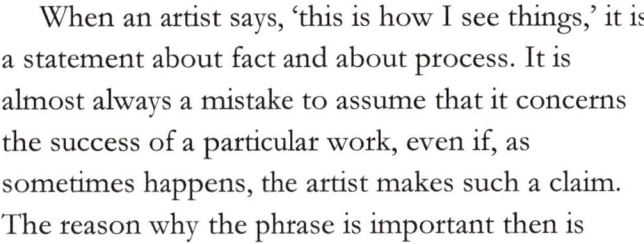

because it rightly draws our attention to the novelty of the artist's perceptions and, therefore, to what might expand our own possibilities for experiencing and understanding the world. In a phenomenological

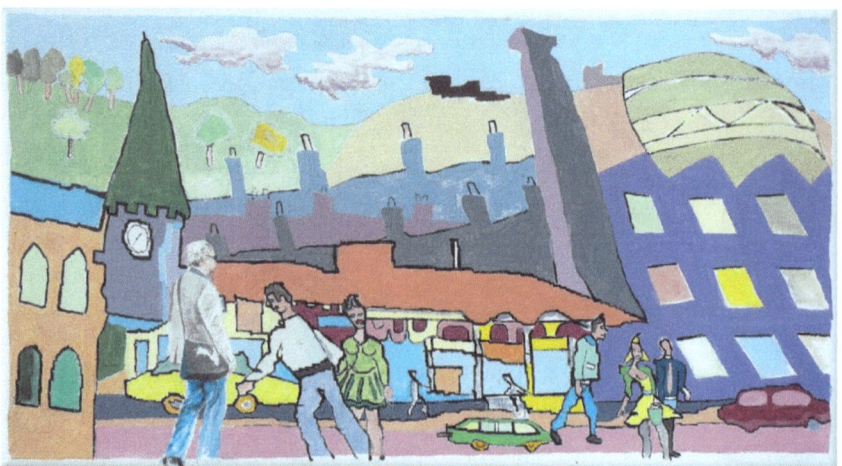

Stepping into Cleartown (2017)
Acrylic on canvas 310 x 560.

sense there is something powerful about being-in-the-world that the artistic process brings to the surface: it is the normally veiled operation of reality making that humans achieve moment by moment without consciously thinking about it. The fact is that reality is always reality *for* someone and, although interrelated, no two realities, from one moment to the next and from one person to the next, are exactly the same. If I may quote myself, 'there is no repetition, nothing happens twice'.[2] Art making partially raises the veil on the reality making operation to present something one can think about.

When I contemplate the *Colourworld* paintings, several features of the world-that-is-seen stand out, and many of them can be seen in Three Lads from the North (p. 15) and in Stepping into Cleartown (left).

The closing in of landscape is apparent and there are two distinct styles of figure representation, one for figures in the scene and one for figures entering it, leaving it, or standing apart from it. These features immediately connote a theatrical space and a hierarchy of actors. One begins to wonder about the relationship between the group and the interloper, trouble maker, appeaser or deserter, and about one's role as spectator and interpreter. Does on-stage action reflect off-stage action and vice versa? What does Davis intend with this scenographic approach? The playfulness of the conceit is enhanced by further features.

To his way of thinking we do not need painting to tell us superficially what things look like. Consequently Davis avoids the illusionistic qualities of naturalism, and chiaroscuro is virtually absent. He emphasizes expressive line and colour field to better capture and fire the imagination, and to transport the viewer to this other world. The theatrical notion 'suspension of disbelief' is called upon by the bold graphic mode of expression. One is reminded of Hockney's stage-related works of the early 80s and his Yorkshire landscapes of the late 90s. Davis also

---

2   Text of two drawings produced for the Lincoln Philosophy Forum, 10 November 2016 (now in a private collection).

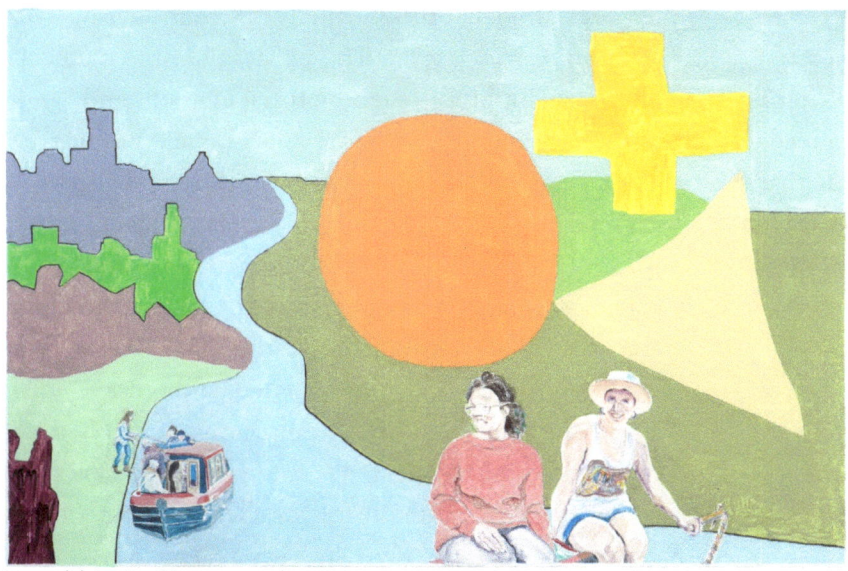

Boat Trip in Cleartown (2017)
Acrylic on canvas 510 x 760.

colour sense. He has a fondness for Surrealism in humour and poetry, but it may be wishful thinking on my part to point to the precedent Surrealist theatre offers for combining symbolism with the compression and expression that is evident in Davis's project. I have to admit that the Theatre of Cruelty and the Theatre of the Absurd of later Surrealism explored darker territory than seems relevant to *Colourworld*. Davis's outlook remains optimistic and his humanistic values emphasize a creative, life-affirming trajectory for the project. This brings us back to the question of the project's substance and to Davis's intentions.

It would be easy to mistake his autobiographical

readily employs figurative excess: he uses distortion and exaggeration, he inverts perspective, and he makes abrupt changes of scale, for example between enlarged foreground figures and a diminished backdrop of buildings. His sense of design is idiomatic in its use of edge and line, and areas of flat colour and texture. He assembles visual elements in each scene with a synecdochal quality, which means that he evokes an expansive, genial world in a series of remarkably economic images.

Finally, although Davis occasionally includes overt symbolism in his work, as in Boat Trip in Cleartown (above), it is thus far a marginal aspect of *Colourworld*, but this may change. De Chirico's metaphysical painting has influenced Davis's approach, as much as Hockney's pure line and

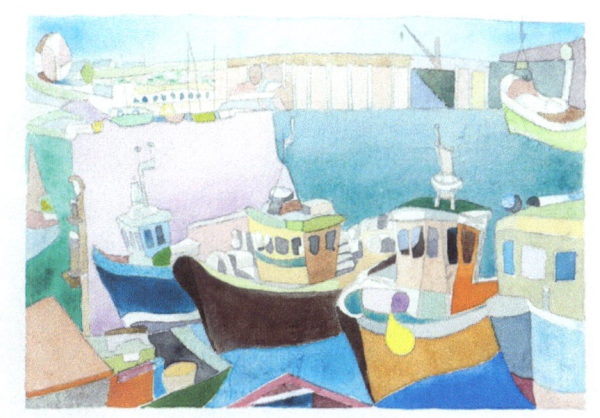

Peaceful Harbour, East Coast (2017)
Watercolour on handmade paper 300 x 420.

references as an exercise in nostalgia, an attempt to recapture a lost sense of belonging. But the *Colourworld* project is no *Odyssey*: there is no heroic return, no quest for the comfort of an idealized past. The vision is forward looking; it reminds us that the world is continually re-invented and re-enchanted simply by our remaining open and being in the moment. The brilliance and magic of reality is there for the making: in a never-ending adventure, experience enriches memory and imagination, as memory and imagination enrich experience.

The world that is seen is, of course, the result of a way of seeing the world. In his art Davis's way of seeing the world distils pure line and saturated colour from the chaos of energy in even the simplest scene, whether observed or imagined. He has explored the two facets of this approach, the linear and the chromatic, consistently over several decades and has brought them together decisively in the *Colourworld* project. The process has the magical effect of amplifying each pictorial element and bringing it into play. Landscapes become interior-like colour fields within which figures and objects, such as the boats in Peaceful Harbour, East Coast (p. 17), form pregnant constellations. The dramatic excesses of overt narrative, conflict, and intrigue are absent as is Expressionistic gesture. Davis draws attention to the subtle, understated, and quirky aspects of place and life by employing controlled compositional means to set scenes that are held in an anticipatory moment for the viewer to absorb.

Do not look to Davis's *Colourworld* for a grandiose sense of historical or political purpose. It embodies something at once more humble, more enjoyable, and more useful: an open honest vision of the bright side of life.

COLOURWORLD

Colin Davis

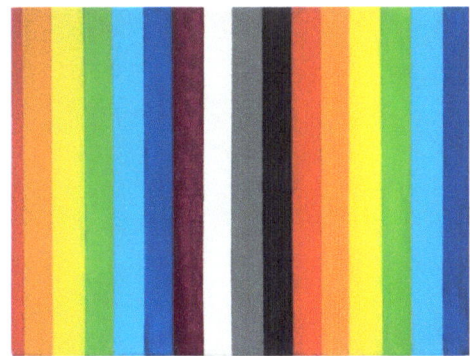

16 (Sensorigraphic Continuum) (2006)
Acrylic on canvas 230 x 300.

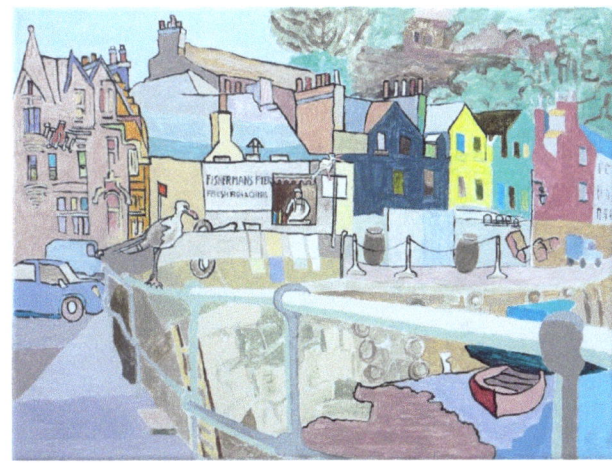

Port on a Scottish Island (2017)
Acrylic on canvas 300 x 400.

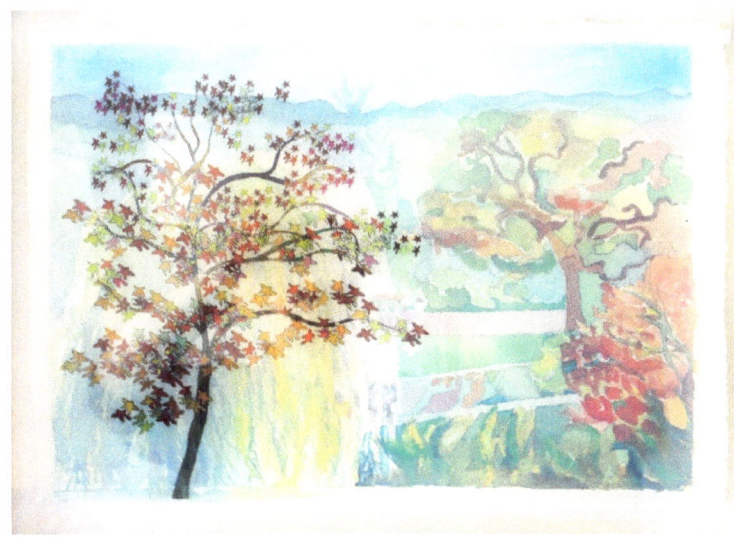

Autumn (2018)
Acrylic, watercolour on handmade paper, and inkjet print
on clear film, image 300 x 420 (frame 420 x 540).

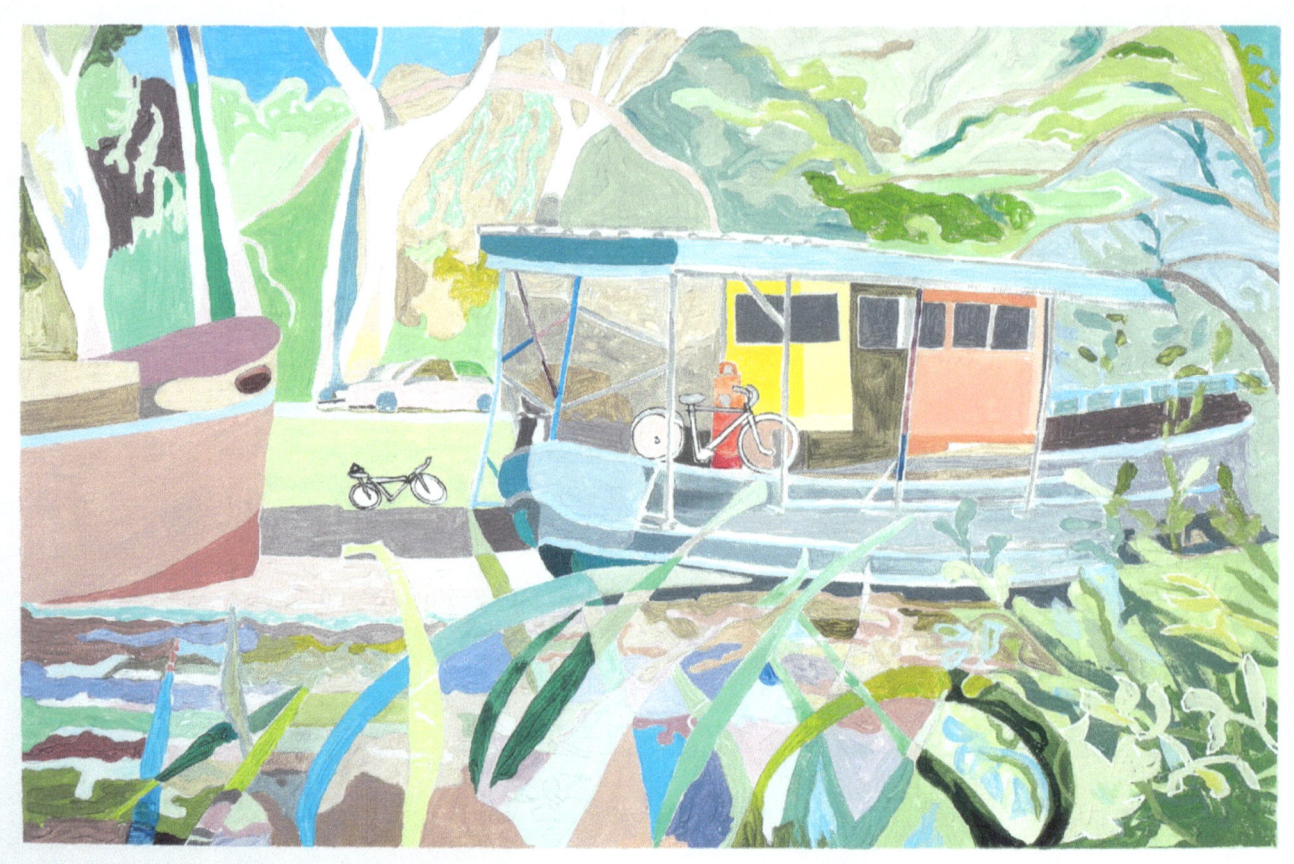

Solitude by the Fossdyke Navigation (2017)
Acrylic on canvas 510 x 760.

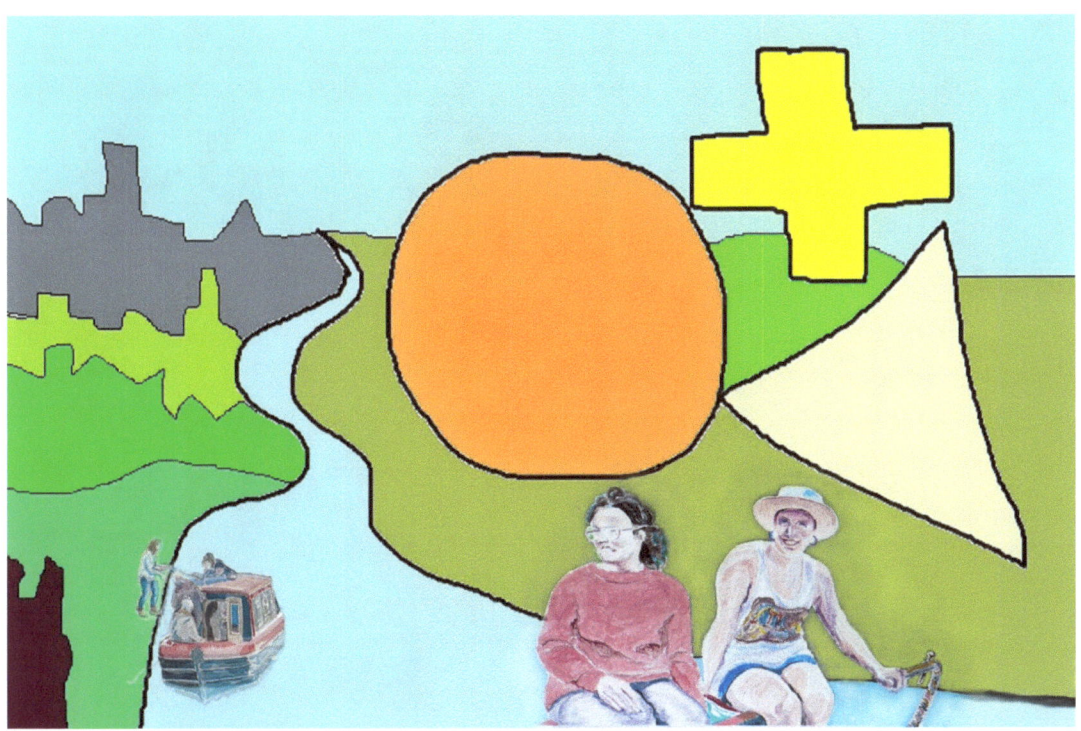

Boat Trip in Cleartown v5 (2017)
Digital print (size variable).

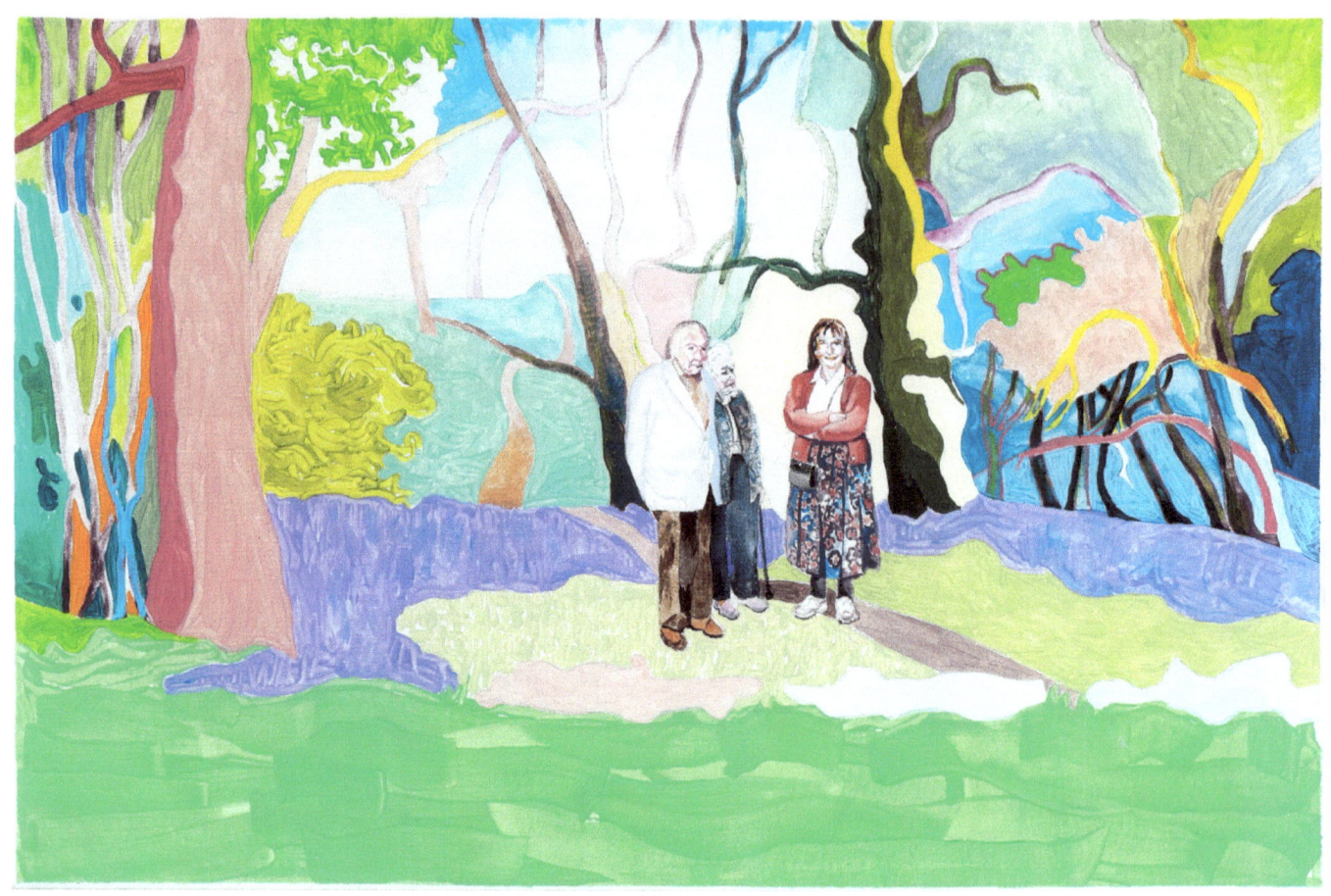

Inger with her Parents in Bluebell Woods (2018)
Acrylic on canvas 510 x 760.

AFTERWORD

I met Michael Blackburn and became friends in 1965 in our first year at Richmond School Yorkshire. In 1975 while students in Leeds we met Colin Davis and soon afterwards began collaborating on art projects. We have remained friends ever since. Graham Freestone, convener of the Lincoln Philosophy Forum, met me when I first attended the Forum in the mid-2000s. I have been a regular participant since 2014.

The *Atmospheric Chambers and Colourworld* exhibition is an important milestone in our artistic careers. It is the first public showing of work which, in both our cases, takes a new direction.

Davis's painting, 16 (originally titled Sensorigraphic Continuum), was the seed that led to the *Colourworld* project a decade later. In it many threads from his past artistic interests and achievements come together for the first time— landscape, drama, memory, pure line, colour field, and spontaneous invention—in a joyous, scenographically imagined programme.

I only returned to full-time art making in 2015. The paintings in the exhibition were produced between February 2017 and February 2018. They represent a unique coalescence of themes, elements, techniques, and emotional responses initially inspired by reading Peter Sloterdijk's *Spheres* trilogy, hence the title: Atmospheric Chambers.

There is no adequate way to acknowledge all of the individuals who have inspired, supported, and spurred on our work. Those that are living know who they are, and those departed we know for what they gave. Our gratitude is deep and sincere. As regards this booklet and the exhibition which occasioned its publication, three people deserve special thanks: Michael Blackburn and Graham Freestone for their generous written contributions, and artist-gallerist Phil Bowman for programming the exhibition, which ran from 3 to 15 April 2018 at the Gallery at St Martins, in Lincoln, UK.

Geoffrey Mark Matthews, March 2018

BIOGRAPHICAL NOTES

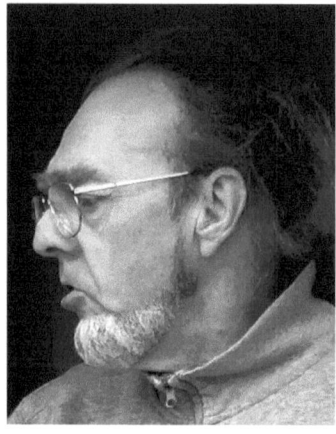 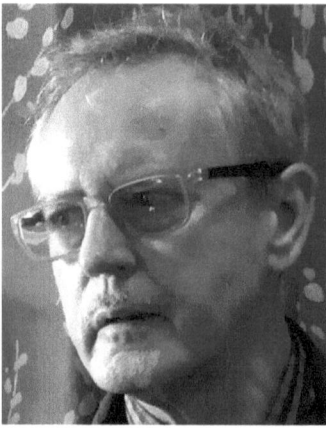 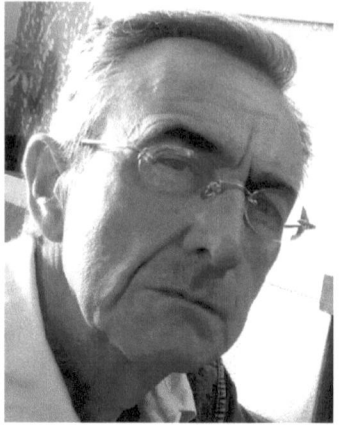 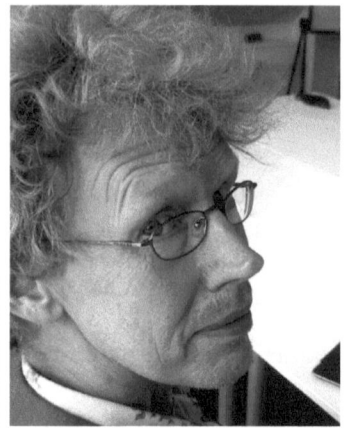

Geoffrey Mark Matthews
began his career as an exhibition designer and worked in a national museum. Subsequently for 28 years he was a university lecturer and mid-career completed a PhD at the University of Hull. He is a poet and writer, and as an artist his work includes drawing, painting, collage, performance art, music composition and free-improvisation, video and digital imaging.

Colin Davis
was educated at Norwich School of Art and Bretton Hall, and enjoyed a 38-year career in special needs teaching. Latterly he completed an MSc at Sheffield Hallam University developing innovative new-technology teaching aids. His visual art has ranged across ceramics, film, drawing, collage, print making, video, digital imaging and painting.

Michael Blackburn
is a poet and writer. He is a lecturer in English and a tutor in Creative Writing at the University of Lincoln. Michael is also an experienced editor and publisher, and an accomplished cross-media artist. Much of his work is archived on-line as part of his long-running Art Zero project.

Graham Freestone
is a philosopher and convenes the Lincoln Philosophy Forum. He runs the Centre for Experimental Ontology, and is co-editor of *Parasol* the CEO's journal. He is also a member of library staff in the University of Lincoln.

www.ingramcontent.com/pod-product-compliance
Lightning Source LLC
Chambersburg PA
CBHW050431180526
45159CB00005B/2501